FLOWER POWER

a love affair with flowers

Design
Leif Södergren

contact: lemongulch@yahoo.com

Photos: Leif Södergren
(except where indicated)

ISBN 978-91-986466-0-3

LEMONGULCHBOOKS
www.lemongulchbooks.com

FLOWER POWER

a love affair with flowers

LEIF SÖDERGREN

CONTENTS

Still Life Ambrosius Bosschaert 1617

INTRODUCTION

I don't think there are many flowers to be found in ancient cave paintings but we have certainly made up for it since then. Poets and musicians find inspiration in flowers. We depict flowers in paintings and on ceramics. We carve flowers into wood, etch them onto glass, forge cold iron into the shape of delicate flowers, we embroider them, we put them on textiles, wall paper, on clothes, and on shoes. We make perfume from flowers. We even make artificial flowers from plastic and silk and decorate cakes with sugar flowers. We even emboss flowers on toilet paper. We have an international network of florists ready to deliver a bouquet of flowers anywhere in the world. If that's not love of flowers, I don't know what is.

And when it is too dark and cold to grow flowers, we make extensive plans for growing them later. As the earth turns on its axis, allowing more sunlight to hit the ground and the days to become longer, we anxiously wait for the first flowers to make their debut. Simply put, we humans are besotted with flowers. We love them to bits.

Great Britain (perhaps more than any other nation) has, with its mild climate, created a nation of dedicated gardeners. They are devoted to flowers and this consuming interest is manifest in the multitudes of flower and agricultural shows all over the country where ordinary people can show up and compete with their masterpieces -- the best flowers (and also vegetables and fruits) in many different categories with colourful ribbons and plaques for the winners. It is both admirable and highly civilised. This book expresses all of the above and my delight in growing flowers and the flower power that, from south to north and east to west, touches us all.

Cream and purple tulips with light blue grape hyacinths, in The Garden Society of Gothenburg.

SWEDISH
SPRING

Scilla in abundance

VERY EARLY SPRING

In early spring when nothing else grows in Sweden and we are well and truly starved for flowers, I keep an eye open for this local private garden where these light blue Scilla flowers seize the opportunity to have free reign of the lawn. I enjoy this delightful floral anarchy while it lasts. Soon this pale blue frolic is gone and the lawn mower will bring back the usual order to the lawn and impose a uniform green carpet below the trees. But the Scilla flowers are happy to have had a chance to bloom and spread their seeds. They gracefully withdraw, ready for the performance next year. They are content. They have had their show.

The Fritillaries flourish, undisturbed by lawn mowers.

CITY WILDERNESS

The owner of this private garden in Gothenburg, an elderly man, lovingly kept the wild character of this patch in the garden, postponing the first mowing of the grass. Not many would be so caring. I always waited for the delicate spring flowering Fritillaries with their checked pattern on the petals. Maybe they felt more loved somehow. They thrived in great numbers and bloomed every spring to their hearts content.

The Garden Society of Gothenburg.

BULBS COME TO THE RESCUE

The Swedish winters are long. Miserably long. When bulbs bloom in St. James Park in London in February, many areas of Sweden are still beneath a snow cover and we must wait a long time for the first signs of spring.

The Vikings were very concerned that the sun would not return after a long winter. They took nothing for granted so they sacrificed to their gods. When the sun returned in spring, they were reassured that their sacrifice had worked.

We might not be as worried as Vikings but many of us do get depressed with so much darkness. When the flowering bulbs that were planted in the fall, pop up, they cheer us up no end. When the colour symphony of bulbs in our parks and gardens explodes in May, we're truly ecstatic.

Orange tulips and daffodils in The Garden Society of Gothenburg, planted in traditional carpet bedding style.

Daffodils in the Liseberg Amusement Park in Gothenburg, Sweden

I WANDERED LONELY
AS A CLOUD

by
William Wordsworth

I wandered lonely as a cloud
That floats on high o'er vales and hills,
When all at once I saw a crowd,
A host, of golden daffodils;
Beside the lake, beneath the trees,
Fluttering and dancing in the breeze.

Continuous as the stars that shine
And twinkle on the milky way,
They stretched in never-ending line
Along the margin of a bay:
Ten thousand saw I at a glance,
Tossing their heads in sprightly dance.

The waves beside them danced; but they
Out-did the sparkling waves in glee:
A poet could not but be gay,
In such a jocund company:
I gazed—and gazed—but little thought
What wealth the show to me had brought:

For oft, when on my couch I lie
In vacant or in pensive mood,
They flash upon that inward eye
Which is the bliss of solitude;
And then my heart with pleasure fills,
And dances with the daffodils.

After the lilac has bloomed, "the period of ecstasy" is over and the growing speed goes back to normal.

Wood Anemones

Bird Cherry (Prunus Padus) When it blooms, it starts the "period of ecstasy".

PERIOD OF ECSTASY

When the summer is short and spring comes with a vengeance, the vegetation explodes and this is called the "period of ecstasy". It takes place between the blooming of the bird cherry tree and the blooming of the lilacs. So by the time the lilacs bloom (opposite) the growing speed has become less frantic.

This is a very special part of spring when the tender green leaves appear and the wood anemones cover the entire forest floor. In the city, on every bench people sit, their faces toward the tender sun for which they have eagerly longed an entire winter.

13

Vincent Van Gogh, Sunflowers

PAINTING
FLOWERS

Rachel Ruysch 1665

OLGA'S FLOWERS

My American/Swedish grandmother's oil paintings were mostly of flowers. With many family celebrations (nine children) there were often large bouquets of flowers to inspire her to paint.

She also learned how to paint Swedish Folk Art (below) and that art form contained a special kind of stylised flower. So did her Chinese lacquer work (below) which she became very good at.

As her family grew, she gifted newlyweds with pieces of furniture with Chinese lacquer work and the Swedish king Gustav V, was given two decorated bridge tables. He used to dine with the family when he visited during the summer. She also generously donated her work to charity, where lotteries of her pieces brought in substantial funds for the Red Cross.

My grandmother Olga with her paintings.

Olga's Folk Art - The inside of a bridal chest.

Olga's Chinese laquer work, detail from a chest of drawers.

Olga's oil paintings were mainly of flowers.

17

FLOWERS IN SWEDISH FOLK ART

Swedish Folk Art or "Dala art" was prominent in the Swedish province of Dalarna 1720-1870. The itinerant painters were strangely fascinated by a flowered vine (kurbits) mentioned in the bible and they used it extensively in their paintings.

The bible was a very central part in people's lives. The local clergyman visited every Swedish home and each and every one in the household was harshly questioned about their knowledge of the bible. So when the itinerant painters looked for inspiration, the bible was there to help. They had no idea what the biblical kurbits would look like so they used their imagination. Each painter had his distinct approach.

These are my paintings done in traditional folk style. The wooden "lunchbox" above is decorated with the traditional "kurbits".

Leif Södergren: The Stockholm Food Hall (Östermalmshallen).
Acrylic on wood (80cm x 30cm).

BIBLICAL INSPIRATION

It is in the book of Jonah (in the bible) that the "kurbits", that fascinated itinerant painters so much, is mentioned. One can see why the story of Jonah interested people. Jonah is disobedient (he had an "attitude") and was argumentative with God.

He runs away and is punished by being swallowed by a whale but is spat out after three days of serious repenting. Jonah finally obeys God's original command, namely to go to the city of Nineveh to exhort the sinful people to repent or face being destroyed by God. The people repent and everybody should be happy. But not Jonah.

Jonah believes that the sinners should suffer some punishment for having been so sinful. Jonah, has the audacity to argue with God about his decision to spare the people of of Nineveh. So again Jonah must be taught a lesson.

The lesson is this: God causes a very fanciful, flowering plant, a (kurbits) to grow up over Jonah so he can sleep nicely under the shade of this large plant. But God causes worms to eat the kurbits so it can no longer shade Jonah. Jonah is disappointed and complains to God about not having a kurbits to shade him. God then tells Jonah, that if he grieves for the loss of this one single kurbits-- how much more would God not grieve over the destruction of an entire city of people, which Jonah thinks God ought to punish.
Hopefully all this has taught Jonah something about God being caring and merciful and not to question his motives. After all, God is God and should not be questioned by mere mortals like Jonah. Lesson learned.

Jonah and the Whale by Leif Södergren. Acrylic on wood (80cm x 60cm).

Jonah has spent a few days repenting his disobedience inside the whale and is here being spat out by the whale. After that, he is on his way to the city of Nineveh to do Gods bidding - to tell people to repent and not sin anymore. If you want a more detailed explanation, there is more to read (left).

19

FANTASY FLOWERS

The Dutch flower painters gloried in absolute precision but artists since, have not felt as constrained to stick to the minute realistic details and have let their imaginations flourish.

Primitive painters like the French artist Henri Rousseau (1844-1910) have always been totally into their own naive interpretation of reality (often ridiculed). He worked as a customs officer and could retire and paint full-time at the age of 49.

The painting on the right titled "The Dream", was painted during his last year.

Donovan O'Malley, artist and writer, has happily made his own interpretation of flowers in this tropical setting.

Henri Rousseau: "The Dream" 1910

The painting depicts the artist's mistress from his youth, surrounded in a jungle containing stylised lotus flowers and other plants. The artist was inspired by what he had observed at "Jardin des Plantes" in Paris.

Panel embroidered in crewel wools on blue linen, possibly originally a chair seat cover ca 1740

FLOWERS
ON
TEXTILES

Josef Frank "Hawaii". Courtesy of Svenskt Tenn ©

Josef Frank (1885 – 1967) was an Austrian-born architect, artist, and designer who adopted Swedish citizenship in the latter half of his life. He was the most prestigious designer in the Stockholm design company Svenskt Tenn (Swedish Pewter). His remarkable textiles are still sold and very popular.

The pattern (left) is called "Hawaii". Josef Frank was inspired by the Metropolitan Museum of Art in New York when he created Hawaii. In the museum he found a remarkable collection of Trees of Life from the north side of the Indian peninsula. The print was designed 1943-1945.

William Morris (1834 – 1896) was a British textile designer, poet, novelist, and socialist activist associated with the British Arts and Crafts Movement. He was a major contributor to the revival of traditional British textile arts and methods of production. The printed textile (right) is called "Snakeshead" and was designed in 1876.

William Morris: "Snakeshead"

Swedish wool blanket ca 1950.

"Sunflowers". Lizzie Montgomery Design.

Chair covering ca 1940.

Portuguese embroidered garment, 1800th century.

Embroidered table cloth (240 cm x 170 cm)

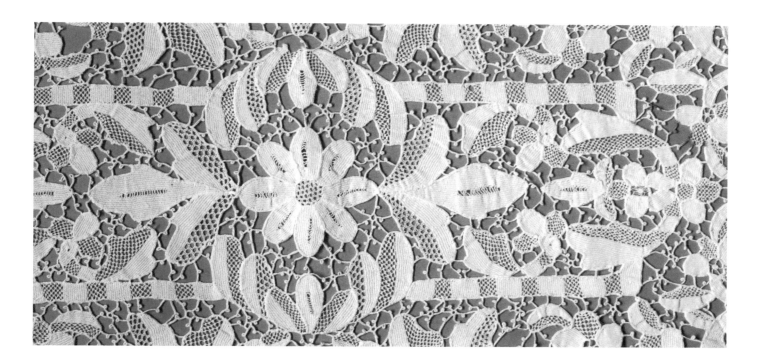

FLOWERS IN THE LINEN CLOSET

For generations, entertaining was always at home. For that reason it has always been important to have quality linen to put on the table.

The embroidered table cloth on the left is very large (240 x 170 cm) and full of embroidered flowers. A work of art. But one shudders at the idea of spots and stains and washing it. Unfortunately, no-one has time for all that busy work these days.

An alternative to a table cloth is using decorative place mats (right), often with floral patterns on top of a highly polished table. As they do at Buckingham Palace.

Richard Sackville, 3rd Earl of Dorset (1589-1624) by William Larking.

FLOWERS ON CLOTHING

We love to decorate our garments with flowers, it has been going on for ages. We never seem to grow tired of it.

Men's ties, ca 1990. From left: St. Michaels, Jaques Estier and Pierre Cardin.

Woman's boot ca 1885. Made from
silk, sueded leather, linen, kid leather.
Photo: LACMA

Contemporary woman's blouse.

32   Rosa centifolia, anemone, and clematis by Pierre-Joseph Redouté

MORE
ABOUT
FLOWERS

My Dahlias 2020

THE DARLING DAHLIAS

Dahlias are popular all over the world but their natural habitat is Mexico and Central America. We still manage to grow them in Northern Europe by digging (lifting) the tubers out of the ground and storing them safely during winter. It is well worth the effort because dahlias produce a stunning amount of glorious flowers in a such a large variety of types and colours.

The British love to grow dahlias and in the south, the frost does not present a danger which is welcome news. With so many growers and so much enthusiasm for this flower, and the wish to show and share, there was a need for some sort of organisation. The National Dahlia Society, established as early as 1881, provides the perfect forum.

The pinnacle for those who grow dahlias for exhibition is The Royal Horticultural Society (RHS) garden at Wisley in September. The show has a dedicated exhibition space run by the National Dahlia Society specifically for the dahlia competitions. This show is very important event for all dahlia growers and dahlia lovers. Just like the Chelsea Flower Show in May, people follow this event from all over the world.

But this is not enough for dahlia enthusiasts. All over Britain there are societies that arrange competitions for dahlias and (of course) chrysanthemums, sweet peas, roses, gladioli etc.!
These competitions have many different levels and prizes, all highly regulated and well run.

It is fascinating, the dedication for these flowers, the organisations built up around the growing, sharing and competing. The interest no doubt forms bonds between people and across generations and social levels. Civilised and admirable.

In Dorset for example, Instagram celebrity, gardener and dahlia grower, Charlie McCormick, who grew up in New Zeeland with agricultural shows, now competes in Britain with his prizewinning dahlias. He is especially fond of local agricultural shows. They are, he says in his Instagram account, *a true celebration of the countryside*.

DAHLIA COMPETITIONS

The photo on the right, kindly provided by Neal Hatch from the Yeovil Chrysanthemum & Dahlia Society in Essex, is one of many awards presented by that particular society. He explains: *"Our society at Yeovil is one of many dotted around the country. We are affiliated to the National Dahlia Society and National Chrysanthemum Society, which means we follow their rule book for judging and are able to award medals for the best exhibits."*

The fine dahlias in the photos you might notice are extremely tall and sturdy besides being perfect in shape and colour. I thought that they might be supported somehow by steel wires, but no such artifice is allowed. Again, Neal Hatch (of the Yeovil Chrysanthemum & Dahlia Society in Essex) explains: *"There are rules set down by the National Dahlia Society, and one of the rules is that there are no supports allowed above the rim of the vase. Typically we use biodegradable (eg 'oasis') florists foam in the vase (in the old days it was newspaper), which makes it easy to stage/ align the blooms. But the long straight stems are down to how well the blooms are grown by the exhibitor and the plant breeding. Show varieties are bred that have particular attributes - like strong stems."*

Photo Brenda Thomas, The National Dahlia Society.

Photo: Neal Hatch from the Yeovil Chrysanthemum & Dahlia Society in Essex

The photos above are kindly provided by the National Dahlia Society. They are from one of their competitions. Photos Brenda Thomas

GROWING AND SELLING DAHLIAS

In 1789, dahlias were sent from the Botanical Garden in Mexico to the Botanical Garden in Madrid. The director in Madrid, Abbe Antonio Jose Cavanilles, cultivated them for a few years and in 1791, he named them "Dahlia" in honour of the talented Swedish botanist Anders Dahl (1751-1789). And from Madrid, they spread to the rest of Europe and the non-arctic world. Now they are in everybody's garden.

In order to satisfy the enormous demand for dahlia tubers, there are professional growers where you can buy from a catalogue, online or via a personal visit. It can be exciting to explore the newcomers in a particular year. Then there are much visited flower shows such as RHS Wisley, where professional growers like "Halls of Haddon" exhibit what they have to offer.

Photo: Halls of Haddon

The dahlias from professional growers might end up in private gardens, like this charming cottage garden in Tissington, Derbyshire, or are even sold abroad. I bought mine this year from a company in Britain. It appears that they were actually grown in the Netherlands. Photo: John Roger Palmour

MY OWN DAHLIAS

Growing dahlias in Sweden is challenging especially with our invasive "murder slugs" as Swedes call them. They are also called the Spanish slug (Arion vulgaris). The last time I planted dahlias in the ground, the slugs ate every new shoot. This year I gave the dahlias an early start indoors and after a long spring inside, I planted them in large containers outside the living room windows. A five centimeter wide copper tape on the containers stopped the slugs from getting up to the dahlias. It all worked very well and I could enjoy the dahlias from inside as well from the garden. The dahlias can be seen left and pps 34 -35.

My dahlias getting an early start indoors.

39

OSCAR WILDE AND LILLIES

When Irish writer Oscar Wilde left his studies in Oxford and settled in London, he had already carefully marketed himself as belonging to the Aesthetic Movement. Charming, well read and witty, he soon had a large devoted audience. His hair was flowing, he dressed and acted flamboyantly and often appeared with a thing of beauty in his hand, like a lilly. That was the image he presented to Americans on a lengthy tour across the continent. Oscar Wilde was received in America like a superstar.

On the subject of lillies, Oscar Wilde once flung a handful of lillies on the ground in front of the renowned French actress Sarah Bernhardt as she got off the boat in Falkstone. She caught on and reluctantly walked over them. And Wilde exclaimed *"Hip, hip hurrah. A cheer for Sarah Bernhardt"* (Matthew Sturgis: Oscar. A Life. 2018)

LILLIES: MAJESTIC AND INSPIRING

I remember being asked by a somewhat pompous person: *"Bring back some flowers, but don't bring any common ones !"* Common? I did not know that there were any "common flowers" !
But I imagine that majestic and fragrant lilies would rank high in such a person's estimate. Lillies are indeed impressive in a vase or in the garden. They have definitely had a distinct influence on art nouveau artists and architects as seen here.

Today I doubt that an architect would design an iron staircase with flowing flowers like the one at the University of Heidelberg (below) but architect Joseph Dorm had no such hesitation in 1905. Also, would anyone else design a tiled, fireplace oven (right) with such floral abandon today?

Earthenware tiled fireplace oven circa 1900, built by Ernst Teichert. Photo courtesy of Instagram @artnouveaudelights.

Spiral staircase at the University of Heidelberg 1905.
Architect Joseph Durm.
Photo courtesy of Instagram @artnouveaudelights.

41

VITA SACKVILLE-WEST AND SINGLE-COLOURED SCHEMES

Vita Sackville-West (1892-1962) was a British author and a very influential garden designer. In 1930 the family moved to Sissinghurst Castle in Kent. It had at one time been owned by Vita's ancestors.

The castle needed substantial renovation and she and her husband, novelist, Harold Nicholson (1886-1968) spent many decades creating the now famous garden at Sissinghurst.

Vita designed a system of garden "rooms" and as you moved from room to room, there were new experiences to be enjoyed. She gave some of these rooms single-coloured schemes. This was very novel and she influenced many other garden designers. She certainly influenced Lawrence Johnston's Hidcote Manor Garden in Gloustershire. It is one of the best-known and most influential Arts and Crafts gardens in Britain, with its linked "rooms" of hedges, rare trees, shrubs and herbaceous borders. There are single-coloured schemes there also and the "Red Border" (far right) is the most famous.

Portrait by William Strang 1918

A white "room" at Sissinghurst. Photo John Roger Palmour

42

Sissinghurst castle. Photo John Roger Palmour

The Sissinghurst garden with it's famous garden "rooms".
Photo Tony Hisgett

Sissinghurst, where the "rooms" often have ornamental urns as a visual contrast to the flowers.
Photo John Roger Palmour

The famous "Red Border" at Hidcote Manor Garden, influenced by Vita Sackville-West. Notice the decorative urns in this garden also.   Photo John Roger Palmour

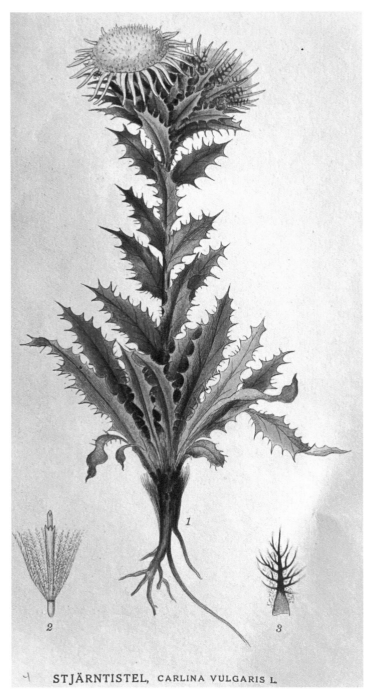

STJÄRNTISTEL, CARLINA VULGARIS L.

LUKTNYPON, ROSA RUBIGINOSA L.

These drawings are from "Pictures from the Nordic Flora 1926" by C.A.M Lindman. He and many others, benefitted from Linné's system for classifying plants.

44

CARL VON LINNE

There is a saying that God created the world, and Carl von Linné (1707-1778) organised it.

A professor at the Uppsala University in Sweden, Linné created a system for classifying and naming nature and in essence, his system is still used by scientists today.

He was creative and curious, was excellent at networking and had contacts all over the world. One of his students, Anders (Andreas) Dahl, did important work and the dahlia was actually named after him (p38.).

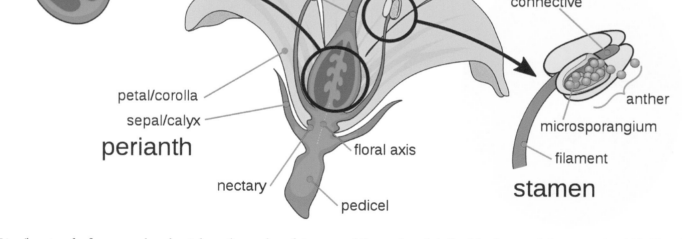

Mature flower

ovules
pistil
stigma
style
ovary
connective
anther
microsporangium
petal/corolla
sepal/calyx
filament
perianth
floral axis
stamen
nectary
pedicel

Linné's system for flowers was based mainly on the number of stamens and the number of pistils of the flower and the manner in which, if not free, they were joined together. Students could rapidly place a plant in a named category.

NAMING ROSES

It is easy to name a rose but much more difficult to hybridise one worthy of naming. Because, as Gertrude Stein once said, *"A rose is a rose is a rose!"*

One of the most famous roses, the hybrid tea "Peace", was introduced right after the end of World War 2. It received a lot of publicity and got people interested in growing roses again, after the long war.

At David Austin Roses in Britain, they told me that they name their roses after literature and poetry which was a great interest of Mr Austin and they also name roses after his family members.

THE QUEEN ELIZABETH ROSE

A favourite rose in my garden is the "Queen Elizabeth" rose (left). It is an exquisite rose surely fit for a queen and has received many awards.

It was bred by Dr. E Lammerts in America and named in honour of Queen Elizabeth II when she ascended the British throne in 1952.

It is described by RHS Plants, as an "incredibly popular and robust rose, which has an excellent resistance to disease. The rounded pink blooms appear in profusion over several months on long stems, which rise up from amongst the dark green leaves.
This tall floribunda rose is ideal for an inhospitable spot and makes a great choice for both novice and more experienced gardeners".

THE ASTRID LINDGREN ROSE

The Astrid Lindgren rose (left) was introduced by Poulsen Roser A/S in 2001. It has a wild rose scent and is described as is an upright, deciduous shrub with distinct thorny stems bearing pinnate leaves divided into glossy, toothed, dark green leaflets and clusters of double, cupped, pink flowers from late spring into autumn.

I am glad that this lovely rose is named after Astrid Lindgren, the author of children's books. She was charmingly down-to-earth, had a great and quick wit and a delicious, playful sense of humour.

She was, in a way, like her famous character "Pippi Longstocking". As an adlult, she always played with her children and in her sixties, she proved to a photographer that she still liked to climb a tree.

FLOWER PERSONALITIES

By Beasley Leffew

Montaigne believed animals have inner lives, and I believe he was right; it seems to me that flowers do as well. We know there is a certain intelligence in the way they present themselves to various insects to ensure pollination; and some carnivorous plants like the Venus flytrap show preparation and planning in capturing their prey.

They know the secret of photosynthesis and how and when to open and close for most efficiency in that process. They know when to release pollen and spores to propagate in distant places. And some are adept at camouflaging themselves from predators.

All this and more suggests an intelligence of a kind that we know little of. And where there is intelligence of a special kind, there must also be cognition of a special kind; and from all this flows personality of a special kind. Flowers live in a dimension foreign to our own, a complex and lively dimension; they live complex and lively existences.

We should recognize their inner life, the personalities they present, and not limit our appreciation of them to their beauty alone.

"This one is a Torch Dancer, fiery, explosive, sending out dangerous rays of sex with every movement, sinuous and swirled at the center and then exploding into unrestrained passion in all directions. She is dangerous but irresistible, she is both the fire and the siren that summons her helpless lover to her flames.
I am reminded of Coleridge: '*Weave a circle around [her] thrice/ And close your eyes with holy dread...*' She is the flame to which the moth is drawn."

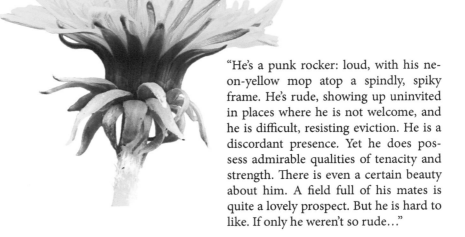

"He's a punk rocker: loud, with his neon-yellow mop atop a spindly, spiky frame. He's rude, showing up uninvited in places where he is not welcome, and he is difficult, resisting eviction. He is a discordant presence. Yet he does possess admirable qualities of tenacity and strength. There is even a certain beauty about him. A field full of his mates is quite a lovely prospect. But he is hard to like. If only he weren't so rude..."

"Now this is a fellow with a fiery heart at the center of his very being. It glows with a smoldering passion and inflames his every thought and movement. He is intense, flamboyant, his very gaze can scorch, his flaming touch can burn. He extends his hot hand to lead you to his enchanted pleasure dome, but beware! Beware! His flashing eyes, his floating hair! You will get burned!."

"Her lipstick is smeared and her gown is a bit tattered at one edge, but in the right light she is still able to turn a head or two. A bit faded, she nevertheless retains some of the old attraction for her gentlemen (and sometimes lady) callers; bees and butterfly admirers. "Oh, in my youth I excited some admiration," she wistfully notes. Some call her Dahlia. I call her Blanche."

"Travel past the exploding purple rays, through the ring of golden shooting stars bursting forth from the center. With lightning speed, accelerate into that dark, mysterious center space to which your eye is drawn. You see? A tiny universe, a dimension alien to human comprehension exists therein. I am eternity in a flower."

"Now this one is channeling Carmen Miranda, the "Brazilian Bombshell" of the 1940's with her crazy headdress, her wildly vivid colors, her suggestively curving green hips as she sways to the samba. She is extravagant, exuberant, an intentionally self-parodying dynamo who is all about the fun of the thing. "Ay Yi Yi Yi Yi, I like you very much," she seems to sing, like Carmen herself."

"This one is a rough fellow, a sailor perhaps, his skin rendered a comely chocolate hue from a thousand suns sailed under the equator. Or he is a longshoreman, a workingman who enjoys his pint with his mates at the end of a long day of labor. Like Mr. Peggoty in David Copperfield, who was also a sailor, you will find him 'rough but ready.' "

"This one, I think, is a young girl dressed in virginal white for her first communion. Her excitement radiates outward from the center of her being like a thousand rays of sun lighting a future into which she hesitatingly, yet trustingly, steps. I've always thought there was something of the naif in white anemones; they look so wide-eyed, shy and disingenuous. I know. It's a lot to ascribe to a flower."

"This one is a grande dame, clad in a flowing gossamer gown of delicate purple. She wears this all the time; it is her color and she is seldom out of this filmy gown in which she holds court at her Mayfair salon for her circle of friends - writers, artists, musicians. She is gracious, a little condescending, generous with the champagne and canapés, amused and amusing. Her coterie includes a wide range of personalities, including the flamenco dancer whom we have met before."

51

FLOWER FRENZY:
THE CHELSEA FLOWER SHOW IN LONDON

In London, during five days in May (on the grounds of The Royal Hospital in Chelsea) something quite spectacular takes place: The Royal Horticultural Society (RHS) arranges their CHELSEA FLOWER SHOW. Garden- and flower lovers from England and visitors from all over the world try to get a peek at the many superb presentations. It is unbelievable how nurseries and garden designers master tricky logistics to have flowers of all kinds ready at peek bloom. They excel and compete in different categories with extremely elaborate arrangements and constructions. One could write an entire book about each such exhibition but I am showing one spectacular example of a designer garden, courtesy of Landform Consultants.

The 2018 "Welcome to Yorkshire" garden by Mark Gregory.

Photo Rachel Warne

Photo Rachel Warne

The 2018 "Welcome to Yorkshire", garden was voted as the BBC RHS "People's Choice Award". It is inspired by the Yorkshire dales and contains a cottage of drystone wall surrounded by flower-filled meadows and a stream. It was crafted by Mark Gregory of Landform Consultants. This is very idyllic and peaceful but not seen here, behind the fence, is a large throng of people from all over the world, trying to get a closer look. It is very impressive, all of it created on a flat piece of ground just before the show opened.
It is only a shame that it all gets taken apart after five days. But the many flower displays would of course, not last past five days.

Only a few of the many fine flower displays Photo John Roger Palmour

FLOWERS FOR MEDICINE

Botanical gardens devote their resources to the study and conservation of plants, as well as making the world's plant species diversity known to the public. These gardens also play a central role in meeting human needs and providing well-being. These are the two oldest such gardens in Britain:

THE CHELSEA PHYSIC GARDEN

In the middle of Chelsea in London, among expensive real estate and behind a brick wall, lies the 3.5 acre Chelsea Physic garden. At one time, this was far outside the city and the perfect place for the chemists (apothecaries) in London to grow their plants which were used as medicine hundreds of years ago.

Being situated right on the Thames (no embankment built then) meant that ships could arrive with plants from plant expeditions from all parts of the world. The walled garden and the southern exposure on the river, creates a special microclimate which is beneficial for exotic plants. There is a grapefruit tree and an enormous olive tree. The garden contains a unique living collection of around 5,000 different edible, useful and medicinal plants that have changed the world.

Growing healing herbs and plants has been an important business for years and the garden was never open to the public until 1983, when it became a charity.

When I visited The Chelsea Physic garden some years ago, many of the volunteers were elderly women and two of the helpful ladies selling books and prints, informed me that the women who worked there, had all at one time had a garden of their own. This arrangement seemed eminently civilised and charmingly British.

Photo:Elisa Rolle CC Attribution. Share Alike 4.0 Int

University of Oxford Botanic Garden. The Magdalen
College tower in the background.

Photo John Roger Palmour

Photo John Roger Palmour

THE OXFORD BOTANIC GARDEN

University of Oxford Botanic Garden, the oldest botanic garden in Great Britain, and the third oldest
scientific garden in the world, was founded in 1621
as a physic garden growing plants for medicinal re-
search.

Today it contains over 8,000 different plant species
on 1.8 hectares (4½ acres). It is one of the most di-
verse yet compact collections of plants in the world
and includes representatives from over 90% of the
higher plant families.

Törngrens Krukmakeri, Falkenberg (Sweden) 1935

56

MORE
DECORATING
WITH FLOWERS

Cast iron window cover downtown Gothenburg.

Details of flowers on two decorative flower pots.

Drawer handle

FLOWERS ON METAL

You would think that metal being such a hard material, the artist or artisan would shy away from trying to make the inflexiable metal look like something as delicate as a flower. But that seems not to be the case at all. Instead it appears to be a welcomed challenge. The fine work on the silver vase below is very fine indeed. Of course there are mass productions like the pressed flowers and the cast iron window cover (left).

Modern architects would sadly, probably never decorate a wrought iron fence like the one below (or like the iron work on the following page).

Made by a Gothenburg
silversmith in an old style.

The School of Design and Crafts in Gothenburg, in Jugend style, by Hans Hedlund 1904.

FLOWERS ON THE STAIRS

The Rookery building in Chicago, was the tallest building (eleven stories) in the world at the time of its completion in 1888.
At the heart of the building, was the light court, a beautiful, light-filled public space. Sunlight from the opening, eleven stories above, illuminated the light court, decorated with elaborate ornamental ironwork.

Photo James Caulfield

John Wellborn Root (1850-1891), one of the architects, blended past and future, combining modern construction techniques with interior and exterior ornament inspired by ancient Romanesque, Islamic, and Venetian designs. Contemporary architecture is traditionally brutally stark and devoid of decorations. But in the 1880's, when the Chicago School of Architecture developed the world's first sky scrapers, they happily decorated their buildings inside and out. In 1975, the Rookery building was listed as a National Historic Landmark.

Staircase with beautifully wrought iron flowers in
the Petit Palais, an art museum in Paris. Built 1900.
Photo Guilheim Vellut (CC Attr. 2.0 Generic)

Staircase with styalised flowers, in House des Majolique in Vienna built
1899.
Photo: Heferi (CC Attribution-share alike 3.0 Austria

FLOWERS ON CERAMICS

The white surface of a newly fired piece of ceramic is a canvas calling out to be filled. And the skilled artists with the many great manufacturers, have over the years often created exceptional pieces. And what has the inspiration been? Flowers!
Who would have guessed?

Traditional Dutch Delft ware. Notice how the flowers are similar to the Folk Art on pages 18-19.

Porcelain plate with the coat of arms of the duke of Clarence 1789. Photo: Andreas Praefcke

Flat bodied bottle 1870-1880. Metropolitan Museum of Art, NYC

Flower vase ca 1897 by Galileo Chini. Photo: Sailko, GNU Free Documentation License

Origin unknown, privately owned

Fireplace tile, Sweden

Kyō stoneware tiered food box with overglaze enamels, Edo period, 18th century. Los Angeles County Museum of Art

Manufacture de Sévres; Sugar bowl with cover ca 1770

Meissen Tea service ca 1745.
Photo: Dadero

Stig Lindberg (1913-1997)

Jewellry box made by Alexis Falize and Lucien Falize 1875.
Metropolitan Museum of Art NYC

65

FLOWERS ON JEWELLERY

They're unescapable!
Bravo!

Brooch Marcus and Co, Ca 1900 Metropolitan Museum of Art NYC
Plique-à-jour enamel, conch pearl, diamond, platinum and hold

Lalique comb
https://commons.wikimedia.org/wiki/User:Sailko

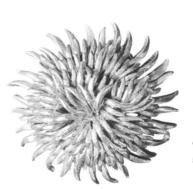

These two costume jewellry pieces
also imitate flowers

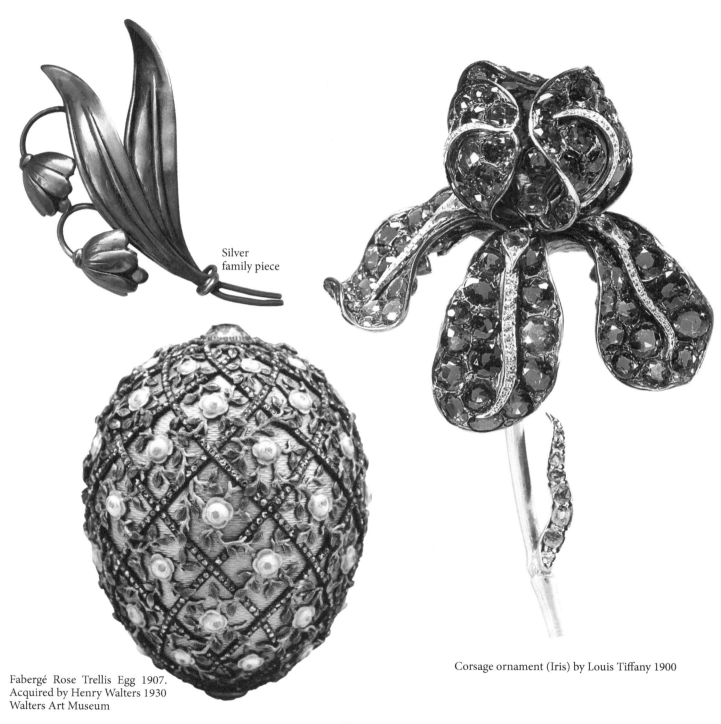

Silver
family piece

Corsage ornament (Iris) by Louis Tiffany 1900

Fabergé Rose Trellis Egg 1907.
Acquired by Henry Walters 1930
Walters Art Museum

FLOWERS ON BUILDINGS

The telegraph company (1912) in Gothenburg, is built in the National Romantic style (above). The inspiration came from medieval and prehistoric nordic subjects. The building displays genuine craftsmanship throughout. Above hammered copper doors (not shown) there are fine leaded glass windows with floral patterns. Above, is the Arts and Crafts inspired fresco ceiling with floral elements.

More flowers are found on this Jugend house in another part of town.

Detail from the Dickson People's Library in Haga, Gothenburg.

This fresco is found on a small building in Gothenburg on Vasa Street, called "The Gnome House" built 1890. The fresco describes gnomes, or "tomtar", busy at work with the various occupations of the two main occupants who lived in the house, a newspaper editor and a photographer. The gnomes are entwined with floral windings. A "tomte" or gnome, was in Swedish folklore a small, usually benign creature that looked after the farm animals.

This unusual facade is from "The Majolica Building" in Vienna, constructed 1889 by Otto Wagner. It is covered with glazed earthenware tiles in floral design. Photo: Greymouser CC Attribution-Share Alike 3.0 Austria

FLOWERS
ON WOOD

Chest with Flowers 1844, intarsia on wood by an anonymous artist.
Most likely a marriage chest of the brides Schnecke and Zimmann.

Sculpture by Amalia Årfelt at Helgö island near Stockholm, Sweden. Photo: Holger Ellgard CC Attribution-Share Alike 3.0 Unported
I have added some of my own flowers.

Ferdinand the Bull

The Story of Ferdinand (1936) is the best known work written by
American author Munro Leaf and illustrated by Robert Lawson.
The children's book tells the story of a very intelligent bull who
thought it better to smell fragrant flowers than fight in bullfights.
We couldn't agree more.

FOR THE LOVE
OF FLOWERS

The entrance to The Garden Society of Gothenburg.

Traditional carpet bedding.

"The Mist" by Gusten Lindberg 1885

FLOWER PARADISE DOWNTOWN

The Garden Society of Gothenburg is situated directly downtown, along one of the many canals/motes, offering lovely walks in the park or in shaded woodlands. The park is one of the best preserved 19th century parks in Europe. There is also a Palm House, the only one of its kind in Sweden. It was inspired by the one in Kew Garden, London. Many cities around the world have similarly centrally located parks and they are essential places for our well being, where we can relax and enjoy flowers to our heart's content.

The Garden Society has one of the finest collections of roses in Northern Europe. There are many seating areas where you can enjoy the roses in the sunshine.

These women have managed to find a very secluded place among the rose bushes to have their "Swedish fika", tea or coffee and something to eat. I did intrude somewhat when I took the photo but I don't think they were much disturbed. It just looked so cozy.

THE PINK HOUSE:
A SPECIAL LOVE OF FLOWERS

There are many private gardens in Gothenburg that contribute to the green enjoyment of the city. This is a favourite of mine. One feels very much a part of this very narrow garden that is wide open to pedestrians and passengers travelling by on the number five tram.

The garden has a special charm and there is a loving and winning whimsy in the placement and choice of a great variety of plants. The owners are often seen lovingly tending to the plants. For years the garden was attended by an elderly couple. Lately I have seen only the elderly woman, assisted by her middle-aged son.

The frontage consists of only a few feet and yet there is a majestic Magnolia hugging the pink facade. Not many people would allow a large tree to block an entire window like this but that is what makes the owners seem so special.

There are very few pink houses in Gothenburg except for the buildings at the Liseberg Amusement Park nearby, where all the buildings have been traditionally pink since 1923.

I asked the elderly lady if they had been inspired by the pink buildings at Liseberg, but she answered: *"No, my husband just liked the colour pink"*.

It is amazing how the owners have managed to plant so many beautiful rose bushes (they obviously love pink) in this limited space.

Two slim-stemmed primroses (below) flank the small gate that opens up to an old fashioned gravel walk. The soft magenta coloured rose petals shine against the grey/green foliage.

In August the flowers have turned into beautifully red, rose hips. A nutritious treat for the birds in winter.

ANEMONE JAPONICA
by Beasley Leffew

They look expectant, these little flower faces,
As if anticipating an answer,
Alert for what may be forthcoming
From some future knowledge.

Late bloomers, summoning summer into fall,
After others have achieved their summit,
They follow in quiet beauty,
Bringing light to the fading season.

Here, through long coming and brief flowering
They trail with their questioning faces.
What is the question, or is it prayer?
And will the answer toward which they bend

Come before they join the others
To lie late in long winter?

Later in the summer, the light pink (of course) Japanese anemones thrive in the narrow frontage gently shaded by the magnificent magnolia tree. The tree and the plants seem to magically fit and thrive on these few feet of fertile and well tended soil.

These red lillies (above) multiplied and flourished amazingly in a rectangular IKEA storage container.

BALCONY FUN

For many years I got carried away with my flowers on the balcony until there was hardly any place to sit.

If one uses professional potting soil and time-released fertilizer and water regularly, you have happy flowers that perform wonders for you. The dahlias were up to 6 feet high.

There was some concern about all the weight from the heavy pots so I tried using plastic containers where I could. But it was great fun, and the best of it all was that there were no slugs to bother me way up there.

MY NEW FLOWER BED: A LESSON LEARNED

I had long been thinking of making a more beautiful transition between the lawn and the wilder part of our country house. Inspired by a gardening book, I thought a half circular flower bed consisting of three parts would be perfect. The additional flower bed meant more weeding, but who cares when you are young and fit?

I dug and turned the turf during an Easter vacation. Rain did not stop me, nor the wet snow that came later in the day but I finally got the first stage finished.

Weeks later when the flower beds were finished, I bought some new plants but mostly I moved plants from other places of the garden. Little did I know that the pink flocks I got from a neighbour had traces of the invasive Bishop's Weed. The plant was introduced to Sweden by monks as a medicinal plant and it has caused trouble for gardeners ever since.

The "evil" Bishop's Weed that ruined everything

My new half-circular flower bed in three parts at the height of summer.

The flower beds flourished all summer long until the next summer when I was hit by a very nasty and long lasting lumbago back problem. I was no longer able to keep up with the weeding. The summer went by and I could not do any weeding at all and frustrated I saw the Bishop's weed take over my new flower beds. Mother Nature was fighting back my attempt to impose my own order. Had I been able to weed, I would have won the battle. But I appeared to be losing, especially as Mother Nature had the ferocious Bishop's Weed on her side. As I got better, I managed to somewhat keep up with the fight, but in the long run it was a losing battle.

Out in the Swedish countryside, nature does not tolerate any bare ground, seeds land almost immediately. Birch trees or weed trees soon sprout if grass is not cut or grazed, and your house is soon surrounded by trees if you let your guard down.

So yes, I learned a lesson from my little endeavour. Yes I got sufficiently humbled and realised how insignificant I was in the greater scheme of things -- Lesson learned !

SEND ME SOME FLOWERS

Flowers help us to become more human. If one does not know how to apologize to a friend or a loved one, flowers are there to help. They bridge a gap and make it easier for us flawed human beings.

We have built up a world wide net of florists that at any moment can send a bouquet of flowers to anyone around the globe (almost). And that is quite an accomplishment.

"You never send me flowers, Clive."

For a retired person who stays at home a great deal of the time, love and support from friends and relatives is of course welcome, but a bouquet of flowers is a reminder that someone has put their money where their mouth is.

My mother Gunilla who loved her flowers.

A SEA OF FLOWERS FOR THE PEOPLE'S PRINCESS

I lived in Kensington for a week in the aftermath of princess Diana's tragic death and it was an unreal feeling. People kept coming on buses and poured up from the underground in a steady stream, day after day. There was a general uproar and conspiracy theories abounded. The press in big headlines, finally begged the Queen to speak to the people and when she did, things calmed down. The funeral was watched by 32 million in Britain. Millions more watched around the world.

People all over the world were stunned and sat glued to their television sets, insatiably absorbing every second of televised footage of princess Diana's dramatic and tragic death during a high speed car chase in a car tunnel in Paris.

It was a set of special circumstances that had been going on for years, that worked together to create this public grieving of epic proportions, reminding one of the frenzied aspects of the Eva Peron cult in Argentina.

The press had delivered a steady narrative of the beautiful Diana Spencer and her fairy tale marriage to the British prince Charles. An endless amount of photos of the shy, withdrawn and vulnerable, yet inviting young princess, were cabled around the globe on a daily, yearly basis. After happiness came unhappiness and then betrayal, confessions and vilifications - elements that ordinary people absorbed liked sponges.

When it looked like the princess was finally moving into a new life and marriage, her life was brutally and shockingly cut short and the public was not prepared for that. In London people went to Kensington Palace, the residence of the princess and they did what we do when we grieve, they brought flowers. The mountain of flowers grew and grew as people kept coming for months.

Diana, Princess of Wales
1 July 1961 – 31 August 1997

SPECIAL MEMORY: QUEEN OF THE NIGHT

The flower of the night-blooming Cereus, blooms for one night only. In the morning the flower has shrivelled. Our garden in San Diego had several of these plants and when we came home late and walked into the jungle-like garden, there was sometimes the most lovely fragrance, permeating the still, ocean-cooled, Southern California, evening air.

When we moved to Sweden after six years, I brought a slip of the night blooming cereus and I started many plants from it. But they never bloomed like they did in California. Something about central heating I think.

Years later when we lived in the country, I gave the plant to our closest neighbour, Alice, who lived some distance down the road She was a woman of great integrity and kindness, a person in whose care, plants tend to thrive. Sure enough, Alice found the right spot inside her house and soon the plant became voluminous and produced flowers regularly. She had never been abroad and was therefore thrilled at this exotic flower. She stayed up late to watch it bloom. Those nights were big events for her and she told us with great joy about her "Princess of the night" as she called it. Such a sweet memory - especially now when our shy Alice is no longer with us.

Above: The garden in San Diego and a photo of dear Alice (right).

1. The **bud of the night-blooming Cereus** is large and strange looking.
Photo: Summita Roy Dutta - CC Attribution-Share Alike Int 4.0 license

2. The **fantastic bloom** that lasts only one night.
Photo: Shamarama64 - CC Attribution-Share Alike 4.0 Int

SPECIAL MEMORY: ROSES IN A JAR

One of the nicest food gifts I ever got was a jar of "slatko", a rose petal preserve (or rose petal marmalade) from former Yugoslavia. People there make "slatko" (preserves) from the choicest fruits and berries of the year and serve it in a very special way.

When guests arrive, there is the jar of slatko together with a jar of many small spoons. People then take a small spoon and put it in the jar of slatko to sample it. It is quite sweet so a glass of water is offered. The used spoon is discarded and a new one taken for a second taste and so on.

I had often spoken to the young cleaner at my job, who had fled the war in Yugoslavia and taken a cleaning job in Sweden as so many refugees did in those days. He had a technical education and would obviously move on with further studies (he now works as an engineer). It was interesting to know about the traditions in his homeland and one day he brought me a jar of his mother's slatko. She had sadly not seen him for a long time but wanted him to have something from home.

I was moved to be given one of these jars of delicious rose petal marmalade in which his mother had preserved the sunshine and rose petal fragrance from their country.

A very special gift.

Photo: John Roger Palmour

SMELLING
LIKE FLOWERS

We sometimes put flowers in our hair, we decorate our clothes, furniture, ceramics with flowers. And we also, occasionally, enjoy smelling like them.

Flowers were originally the main ingredients for what has developed into today's perfume industry. The world's first-recorded chemist is considered to be a woman named Tapputi, a perfume maker mentioned in a cuneiform tablet from the 2nd millennium BCE in Mesopotamia. She distilled flowers, oil, and calamus with other aromatics, then filtered and put them back in the still several times. In ancient times people used herbs and spices, such as almond, coriander, myrtle, conifer resin, and bergamot, as well as flowers (Wikipedia).

British Rococo perfume vase; circa 1761;
soft-paste porcelain; overall: 43.2 × 29.2 × 17.8 cm;
Metropolitan Museum of Art

Saffron harvest, Iran

EATING FLOWERS

We love the way flowers look and we depict them in various ways and sometimes we also consume them. Many flowers can be used in salads and one can fry zucchini flowers. The saffron crocus flower is much sought after for its spice.

SAFFRON

Saffron, is harvested from the strands inside little crocus flowers and used for the extremely popular and expensive spice. That little blue crocus is a big industry.

CAPERS

Another very popular flower to eat, actually the bud of the flower, is found on the caper bush (Capparis spinosa) also called Flinders rose (left).

The plant is best known for the edible flower buds (capers), used as a seasoning. They are usually eaten pickled and consumed all over the world.

Pickled capers

The standing (grave) stones at Li, Fjärås, Sweden, date back to the early iron age.

FEED THE BEES

The symbiotic relationship between plants and bees is one that has long benefitted mankind. Plants need bees for pollination, which in turn benefits humans with the crops that are produced.

Bees pollinate a staggering three-quarters of crops that produce the food we eat. The loss of pollinating insects could threaten our own food supply. Loss of habitat has, sadly, increased in recent years. Clearing of land, a lack of bee-friendly flowers in gardens, use of herbicides and increased prevalence of parasites such as mites, have all contributed to fewer bees.

DELICIOUS WILDFLOWERS
TO FEED OUR BEES

1. Cornflower Centaurea cyanus
2. Common Toadflax Linaria vulgaris
3. Common Poppy Papaver rhoeas
4. Corn Marigold Glebionis segetum
5. Cowslip Primula veris
6. Meadow Cranesbill Geranium pratense
7. Musk Mallow Malva moschata
8. Oxeye Daisy Leucanthemum vulgare
9. Chamomile Matricaria chamomila
10. Night Flowering Catchfly Silene noctiflora
11. Red Campion Silene dioica

Source: https://feedthebees.rowsehoney.co.uk

Read more: 100 Plants to feed the bees
by The Xerces Society

Wildflowers provide lots of the essentials that bees need to thrive; food in the form of nectar and pollen, as well as places to shelter and rest. Most wildflower species have single flowers which are easier for bees to land on. They have vibrantly coloured petals, and attractive scents, that bees simply can't resist. Instantly recognisable, the Common Red Poppy (above) is a pleasurable sight. This photo is from the Worchestershire Wildlife Trust where they have many traditional hay-meadows.

photo by Tony Hisgett

FLOWER OPPORTUNISTS

We have an almost unhealthy dislike of dandelions. They invade our gardens and some people hate them ferociously. They are of course pushy and invasive. But should we really be so hard on them? Don't we admire achievers, tenacity and success?

Maybe not in dandelions. But a field of dandelions can be quite lovely as seen below. But do we hear any poet gushing over a lovely field of dancing dandelions?

Mr. Wordsworth? Anyone?

Anyway, dandelions are great for the bees and we are supposed to support and feed our disappearing bees. Instagram gardener and protector of flowers, chickens and all endangered species, Arthur Parkinson, thinks that we ought to leave dandelions alone and let them bloom so the bees can have an early source of food.

Maybe food for thought.

Australian writer Stephanie McCarthy on a visit to our forest farm Sweden sings to a field of dandelions.

These dandelions close to downtown in Gothenburg, have been clever to bloom and seed themselves long before the city was ready with their lawnmowers.

FLOWERS AND CLIMATE CHANGE IN CALIFORNIA

Southern Californians have come to realize that they no longer can water their lawns as they used to. Water is now a scarce resource. A recent drought that lasted for many years was a warning signal. With climate change and increased temperatures, fires have struck with a vengeance. There is a keen awareness that something must be done.

Many people have sensibly adapted to using native plants in "dry" gardens and what people have accomplished (here in San Diego) in the photos below and right, is very impressive. Many of these plants are sculptural and substantial and have beautiful flowers even if they tend not to bloom during summer. The plants cope with the summer heat by slowing down.

When it rains in the winter, the hills come alive and it is time to enjoy the wildflowers. The native California Poppy, also the state flower, puts on a show. Wild fuchsias are nice too. There is a tradition for San Diegans to go to the desert and see the flowering plants, many of which have now also been introduced into people's gardens.

Photo of, and by Ricardo H Martinez

Wild fuchsia

Photo: Stan Shebs

California Poppy

This San Diego "dry garden" uses much less water now.

Photo Ricardo H Martinez

Enjoy the wild flowers after a heavy rain at this San Diego beach.
Photo Ricardo H Martinez

Cactus apples or "Prickly Pears".
Photo Ricardo H Martinez

A "dry" garden can look quite verdant and sculptural.
Photo Ricardo H Martinez.

Maria van Oosterwijck. Flower Still Life 1669

GOOD BYE TO ALL THIS

The Dutch masters painted flowers at their prime, when the flowers were at their most sumptuous. Much as we might enjoy flowers at their peak, one is painfully aware of their short life-span. The next day, the sublime serenity might be replaced by collapsed chaos. But artists usually do not depict this unflattering decline. Maybe it reminds us of our own? Best to stay away from that subject perhaps?

But, in the painting on the left the artist, Maria van Oosterwijck (1630-1693) has attempted to be more realistic. The tulip on the right has opened up and is at its most beautiful, but the tulip on the left has begun its decline. Some petals have fallen off already and at any moment, the rest of the petals will lie collapsed below.

There is always an end to everything but the most brutal end comes to our flowering friends from South America, the dahlias, when the first frost comes. We, in colder climates have seduced dahlias into thinking that our mild summer weather is just like their southern native countries so they grow vigorous foliage and bloom until late in autumn. They grow to their heart's content, thinking naively (they are only plants after all), that this is going to go on and on - until wham, the frost kills them. Sorry, we should have warned you, but there it is. A brutal end to your lives. Sorry mates!

But amazingly they don't hold any grudges. If we take care of them over winter in a frost-free place, and replant them, they come back as though nothing has happened. What spirit and character! A class act.

British actress Betty Marsden and writer Donovan O'Malley on a Swedish summer day.

NOT SO FAST!

I want to end this little book about our love of flowers -- on a sunny note by revisiting a very special time in the Swedish countryside, at the height of summer, when flowers flourished and when our dear friend, the British actress Betty Marsden, spent another week with us. Betty, known as the master of a thousand voices, had us all laughing as she had kept everyone in Britain laughing during the 1960's, in the radio comedy "Round the Horn". Donovan O'Malley, writer and my husband (by her side in the picture) had got to know Betty when she was in one of his plays at the BBC. And now she was on her second summer visit to our little farm in Sweden.

Here in this photo we are on the way to our closest neighbours up the road, Olle and Elsa. Donovan is holding a bouquet of flowers that Betty has picked in our garden. Betty loved flowers and she arranged them beautifully in vases and luckily, our garden was filled with flowers.

In Donovan's other hand is a large umbrella just in case there will be rain in the evening. Also, it could be good protection should an elk come too close, there are many of those around and if one gets between a mother and a calf, beware. (These days, wild boars have been introduced into the Swedish landscape, but let's not get into that, especially as these animals can be very dangerous and they can also turn your garden upside down with their tusks.)

When we arrive, our friends who speak perfect English, will introduce us to their visitor and long time friend, Swedish operetta star Berit Bohm. And we are all guaranteed a lovely evening with Betty entertaining us all.

It is my conviction that we live far too much in the present and far too little in the past, and if the skies turn dark, we can certainly brighten our insides with a trip like this, down memory lane to a very special day, in a very special place, with a very special and dear old friend.

Leif Södergren

More books
by Leif Södergren:

GOTHENBURG CLOSEUPS
GÖTEBORG NÄRBILDER
132 colour photos
(English and Swedish)

FOOD & FOLK
Memories and thoughts on food and
those who cooked it, with 180 photos
and illustrations from California,
Sweden and England.
(English)

A GARDEN IN GOTHENBURG
TRÄDGÅRDSFÖRENINGEN
132 colour photos
(English and Swedish)

RESA I TIDEN
(Swedish essays)

NÄRBILDER GÖTEBORG
(Swedish)

MY DARLING OLGA
Folke Jonsson Letters 1909-1961
(English)

THE OLGA & FOLKE
PICTURE BOOK
A Pictorial Companion (140 photos) to
"MY DARLING OLGA"
(English)

OLGA & FOLKE
En bilderbok från en svunnen tid
(Swedish)